HOW TO DETECT LIES, FRAUD AND IDENTITY THEFT

FIELD GUIDE

TRACI BROWN

HOW TO DETECT LIES, FRAUD AND IDENTITY THEFT

FIELD GUIDE

TRACI BROWN

Published by
Traci Brown, Inc.
www.BodyLanguageTrainer.com

Copyright © 2017 by Traci Brown

All rights reserved. No part of this book may be reproduced or utilized in any form or by any means, electronic or mechanical, including photocopying, recording or by any informational storage and retrieval system, without permission in writing from the publisher.

ISBN 978-0-692-83249-3

Published by Traci Brown Inc.
Boulder, CO 80305

Cartoon images by Patrick Carlson
Book design by e-book-design.com

Printed in the United States of America

CONTENTS

Intro 7
    Quick Reference Checklist 8
    The Toughest Survival Situation 9

The Truth About Lies 13

Basic Training 19

Body Language: What to Look For 23
    Head 28
    Hands 30
    Face 35
    Feet 41
    Body 42
    Eyes 43
    Pacifiers 49

Verbal Tells 53
    Tone 53

    Other Voice Quality Indicators 56

    Verbal Patterns Liars Will Follow 56

Interrogation Techniques:

    How to find the truth 63

    Tactics to get to the truth 63

    Verbal Patterns. 64

    Your Demeanor 65

    Environment Set Up 65

How to Detect Identity Theft and Fraud 75

So, You Found a Liar—What Next? 81

    How to Get an Admission. 82

Final Review and Tips 83

About the Author. 85

INTRO

I love listening to lies when I know the truth.
—Unknown

The body can't lie. That's why lie detector tests are fairly accurate and why there are so many police and FBI agents that use body language in their interrogations. Hopefully, the lies in your life are milder than the murders and crimes detectives need to solve. However, you don't have to be a law enforcement pro to detect lies.

The lies in your life may be smaller, but they are still important to resolve. Does your customer really have the budget they're telling you they do? Are they happy with your service or the proposal you gave them? Did that job candidate inflate his résumé? Is that person wanting to get a payday loan really who they say they are? And, most importantly, did the kids eat those chocolate donuts on the counter or did the dog?

Not detecting lies in these circumstances and others can negatively impact your bottom line and your relationships with family and friends. When you know what to look for, you can detect lies for yourself and avoid the pain that comes when you discover the unfortunate truth.

Written as a quick reference field guide, in this book you'll find just what you need to know to survive in the wild and detect the lies in front of you, no matter how big or small.

The US Marine Corps Guide to Survival, Evasion and Recovery uses a quick reference checklist for survival. Using it in your life can help you pay attention to find the truth in your own life. If you're like most people, you pay so much attention to yourself that you forget to pay attention to people around you. And they're screaming the truth at you all the time ... even when their words say otherwise.

QUICK REFERENCE CHECKLIST
Decide to Survive (and find the lies!)

S - Size up the situation, surroundings, physical condition, equipment.

U - Use all your senses

R - Remember where you are.

V - Vanquish fear and panic.

I - Improvise and improve.

V - Value living.

A - Act like the natives.

L - Live by your wits.

The Toughest Survival Situation

Bankers may not lose their lives, but they do have to survive the risk of internal temptation every day. A staggering 86% of bank shrinkage is employee theft with the average take $4,000. The managers with the lowest rate of fraud in their departments take SURVIVAL to a more detailed level. They say:

1. Care about people and trust them but don't ever let the fox guard the henhouse.

2. Know Your People—Don't let automation get in the way of face-to-face communication. Get to know people's financial condition, hobbies, and family. For example, if their kids have a sudden severe illness or they go to Vegas regularly, watch them more closely. Ask more questions when you learn someone's husband is out of work, but they're building a new home.

3. When you find a problem, address it and have a consequence. If you let lies and fraud slide, you send the wrong message

> **Gail Crawford—Bank Manager**
>
> *I had an employee who, we found out, was stealing from her customer's CD accounts. When a deposit came in, she'd take the money rather than putting it in the customer's account. She would call all her customers to take care of their needs before she went on vacation so they wouldn't call anyone else while she was gone. We only found out when the customers came to cash in their CDs. They had no money in the account! Here's a tip: make sure nobody takes care of a customer exclusively.*

Remember that people lie all the time—even you! When was the last time you were having a horrible day when an unsuspecting person asked how you were doing? Did you respond "Okay" or "Fine"? Yep! You're a liar, too.

Throughout the book, you'll find stories from people who have survived lies in the wild. You'll learn as much from them as you do from the techniques discussed in the text.

Heads up! Lie detection isn't all about incriminating others. It can be a window into their world and a real opportunity to make their life a little bit better. Does your husband really want chicken for dinner? Maybe not, even though his words say he does.

How to Detect Lies, Fraud and Identity Theft

By the time you finish this field guide, you'll be seeing the world with new eyes and hearing with new ears, well on your way to becoming a human lie detector. One thing is certain, you'll never experience the world the same way again.

Know your people. They're on Facebook, too:

Ryan Crissey—Daycare Owner

All my funny stories involve employees missing work, claiming to be sick, in a car wreck, etc. Then, they bust themselves on social media. One even sent us pictures of "her" wrecked car. A quick Google Image search showed that the picture was taken in Pennsylvania two years prior.

"Call me Suzy"—State Association Board President

I was the president of a state association board. I had one board member who begged me to be on the board but then decided she didn't like to go to board meetings. And, she didn't make a secret about it. There's an unspoken requirement that you go to all the board meetings, no matter what, unless there's an emergency.

About a week before the meeting, I saw her at a friend's house, and she told me she wasn't going to the board meeting because someone was coming over to paint her house and she needed to be there. She was too quick to respond. I didn't believe her.

I reminded her about the rule and she proceeded to fuss about having to go. She didn't show up at the meeting. Instead, she posted pictures on Facebook of her glorious trip to the mountains to view the fall colors.

During my time on the board with her, I learned she is very proud of being belligerent. So, I made the unspoken rule written and it included specific consequences including the threat of removal from the board "if meetings are missed for any reason other than an emergency." I'm waiting to see what emergencies she'll cook up.

THE TRUTH ABOUT LIES

Ask no questions and you'll hear no lies.
—James Joyce, *Ulysses*

The ability to detect lies is hard-wired into your physiology—it's what has allowed humans to survive for millions of years. In ancient times, knowing if you could trust someone was, often, the difference between life or death. Your natural instincts are still there. You feel them as hunches. But in this day and age it's easy to discount feelings. So let's put some science behind that hunch.

Until 1929 when the first crime lab opened, all you had to rely on were the feelings you had about someone. You've probably said, "There's something about that guy that's just not right." Now, the science has evolved, and you have the study of body language to back up those feelings and give yourself a little more proof.

Some people are great liars and are guilt-free. These are individuals without a moral compass or those who are mentally ill. Others have an overwhelming sense of guilt when they lie. How do you differentiate between these two types?

Studies have shown that when people are more focused

on the reward of what they have to gain or lose rather than the costs, the lies flow freely. And, the more power they have, the more they typically have to gain or lose. That power can also make them feel they're less likely to be caught. So, do powerful people lie more? Absolutely.

For example, there are fewer body language 'hot spots' or tells from politicians in debates. The signs are exponentially smaller with more experience practicing scripts, but they're still there. Those lies are hard to completely camouflage even with rehearsal.

A little knowledge can be dangerous. As you learn more, be mindful of incriminating someone based on one movement or gesture. Don't do that!! The FBI teaches that it's best to make your decision based on a combination of tools. It's important to take all factors into account — body language, words, tone, even timing—and how they weave themselves together to tell if someone is lying or not. It's an art and a science.

The best FBI interrogators have an 80-85% accuracy in lie detection and don't use opinion. The average person on the street has a 50% accuracy just using gut feeling which means it's based on opinion. That's about as accurate as a coin toss. My goal for you is to move into the space where you transcend your gut level and detect lies accurately more than 50% of the time by using objectivity. That's when you'll start to see some real results in your business and personal life.

Is it a Power Lie?

Mary Kelly—Economist and Retired Chief of Police, Naval Air Station, Hawaii

We'd had some problems when I took over as police chief. My cops were not always the most upstanding citizens. As a result, many people thought they could, when stopped by them, say the cops were doing something wrong, fight the ticket, and win. And, in many cases, they would because that had worked previously.

I needed to change the environment for my cops so, when they wrote a ticket, it would stick. One of the things I did was equip my cops with sound-activated audio recorders. This was before all the fancy technology now ... before cell phones. It was very new technology. In the beginning, my cops didn't like it, thinking I was checking up on them. But, I knew people they stopped were making up things, lying in court, and winning.

In one instance, a fairly senior person got pulled over on the base. He got out of his car, screamed at my officer, called him all kinds of names, told him it wasn't going to stick anyway, and threatened his career, saying "wait till I get hold of you. I'm going straight to your boss; you can't do this to me ...."

Unbeknownst to him, the audio recording had activated, and we had his entire tirade as well as my cop's reaction on tape.

The man who'd been stopped called me, ranting. I asked him to come over with his boss and we'd have a conversation. I said, "Tell me exactly what happened." Of course, his version of the story was completely different than what I had on tape. He said he never got out of his car; he never called my cop a name; and never threatened his career.

I wanted to make sure the hole was big enough to where he could bury himself. I said, "Just to be clear, this is specifically last Tuesday at 10 am on that road, and this is the cop who pulled you over. Is that correct?"

"Oh yeah. And he was awful."

"Did my cop do anything else that could be misinterpreted in any way as being unprofessional?"

Then, he launched into this whole other story that was completely made up.

When I said, "Did you, by any chance, know that my cops are all equipped with audio sound recording devices?" His face dropped.

He said. "I don't know what you mean."

I said, "This is the version we got on tape" and I pressed play. I sat there with him and his boss; the boss was getting madder and madder because he'd lied to her, too. Here she was putting her neck out for him and he lied.

At the end, I said, "Would you like to revise your statement?"

He said, "Well, I guess it could have happened that way."

I said, "No. Not good enough. Here's what's going to happen now. You're going to tell your boss sitting right here that you lied. Then after we do that, I'm going to bring my cop in, and you're going to apologize."

And, then I said, "What are you going to tell the rest of your department?"

He was a senior guy, and I wanted to let the rest of the 300 people he was in charge of to have some respect for my cops. He said the right thing. "I'm going to tell them not to be bad to the cops."

I said, "Thank you very much. This was a good learning experience for all of us, wasn't it?".

If people have a history where the lying works, they're going to continue it because bad behavior gets rewarded.

(That's in my book Master Your World: 10 Dog-Inspired Leadership Lessons to Improve Productivity, Profit and Communication; Rule #1 is to reward good behavior because you get the behavior you want just like with your puppy. And, don't reward bad behavior because you'll get more of it. In this case, that had been happening. But, no more after this incident.)

BASIC TRAINING

Sometimes you can learn things from the way a person denies something. The choice of lies can be almost as helpful as the truth.

—Laurell K. Hamilton, *Guilty Pleasures*

Why People Lie

Goal-Directed Behavior (to get what they want)
Low Probabilities of Detection
Minimal Consequences of Detection

Types of Lies

Lies come in many forms. In the wild, you'll find all these. Make sure you investigate for all types:

Exaggeration—An attempt to magnify or overstate attributes, accomplishments, or events beyond fact

Fabrication—An attempt to make up nonexistent facts or attributes

Minimization—An attempt to under-report or reduce to the least possible degree any perceived negative fact, event or attribute

Omission—An attempt to leave out critical facts or information perceived as harmful (or irrelevant) to the individual's position

Deceptive Denial—An attempt to refute or maintain that a statement of fact is in error or an event did not occur.

Who lies more?

Women are the best liars. And, they're also the best lie detectors. Their ability doesn't have to do with gender per se; it's more that they're naturally curious and, naturally, have more to lie about, e.g., You look great today!

Women tend to commit crimes that are of the brain and mouth.

Men strong-arm their crimes.

Studies show that financial need is not an indicator of a propensity to lie. It's more likely to be integrity (or lack thereof).

The older you are, the better you are at lying and, also, at detecting them.

Whenever men have a problem, it's a woman's fault (and it's a lie, too!)

Liars will point out their honesty. Honest people don't need to point it out.

Strange stories are usually untruthful, but not always.

When something just feels off…

Nanci Allen

The phone at home would ring at random times and, whenever I answered, no one was there. I kept mentioning it to Bob, my boyfriend (not his real name) and he said I should probably call the phone company; there might be a short in the line. Shrug ... okay, I can live with a short ... for a while. Finally, I said to myself, I'm not sure I buy this "short" idea so I called the phone company. I was told unequivocally it was impossible for a short to cause this to happen. Hmmm! This guy was a little slippery many years ago, but I can't say if I saw a change in behavior or if I just felt something was off. As this "short" escalated, I became convinced that it was "another woman" calling for him. This was before the cellphone was a part of daily life. And then one day finally, rather than hanging up for the umpteenth time, I said hello, and hello again and finally who's calling? A timid little voice asked for Bob. In less than a week he was no longer living in my house!

This same guy told me he fought in the Viet Nam war and told stories about walking through the jungle forests of bamboo and how frightened he was. I fell for it. When his mother came to visit, I mentioned to her how concerned she must have been when he was over there. She laughed and said, "Concerned? HAH, he never left the US; he was stationed in the Coast Guard nearby.

Bob was a habitual liar and is the one who motivated me to dial in on liars—he was good—better than most politicians.

BODY LANGUAGE: WHAT TO LOOK FOR

You may tell the greatest lies and wear a brilliant disguise, but you can't escape the eyes of the one who sees right through you.

—Tom Robbins, *Villa Incognito*

It takes a lot of thinking and energy to lie. That's the reason body language can be relied on to indicate deception. Words are the easiest to control, much less so for tone and body language. Liars not only have to think about the tale they're telling but, also, have to attempt to generate the appropriate emotions and body language that goes with it. And, they do all this while they're judging how they're being received. They go into cognitive overload when these things, that are usually on autopilot, have to be consciously performed. Body language is what usually goes haywire.

One of the most important hot spots to watch for is the timing of someone's gesture. Do they gesture slightly before they speak or slightly after? Truthful people gesture just before they speak. Liars gesture just after they start speaking. This is subtle but worth watching for.

Now that you're looking for when they gesture, take a look at some of the common signs of deception. It's important to use these gestures only as clues, not taking any one as a definitive sign of lying. To spot a liar, you're going to want to look for clusters of signs or hot spots, a tightly grouped series of gestures. When you see three or four during the same sentence, you'll know someone's pants are likely on fire.

Before judging anyone's behavior, it's vital to get a baseline on them. This is to understand how they usually behave. When you compare them to themselves, you get a much more accurate assessment of deception or truth. Then, when you see major shifts, you know you've got a hot spot.

Baselining

Jenny—Vice President of a Design Firm

I have an employee (let's call him Donny) who lies all the time. He lies about what he thinks about things— he tells other people that he thinks different things. And, his body language tells the tale. When he lies, his eyes close to the point they are half open; he shakes his head "no" and he takes a half step back.

One day I caught him red handed. We had a new client and needed to get information and documents from them so we could start work. I asked Donny to collect the info. A week later, I asked Donny where the documents were. Because I knew his baseline, I watched as his eyes narrowed and he shook his head, taking a step back. He said he e-mailed three times, called once, and the client wasn't responsive. He showed all his typical signs and, this time, I knew he was lying because I was able to get into our e-mail system and see that he hadn't sent the e-mails.

> **Nora Burns—Human Resources Executive, Undercover HR**
>
> *I play a lot of poker at the casinos. And, I've begun to run into some of the same players. They're regulars. I've noticed they all signal when they have good hands, and I don't think they know they do it.*
>
> *The easiest one to read is a guy who will shuffle his stack of chips in his hand until he gets a good hand. Then he stops. Another will bluff by putting an extra $100 on the edge of the table to buy chips for the next round, signifying that he's going to lose all his money in the current game.*

To baseline someone you've just met for the truth, just ask two simple questions:

1. "How do you spell your first name?"
2. "Where do you live?"

These will probably give you truthful norms and an idea of how they behave when they're telling the truth.

Looking for deviations from the body language exhibited during their answers to future questions will enable you to find hot spots and the lies they're covering up.

Connie McSwain—Bank Manager

I had to audit several banks on a regular basis but never told them exactly when I was coming. I always knew if something was amiss if I glimpsed people scrambling as they saw me walk in the door.

BODY LANGUAGE TELLS

Head

Shaking head no and nodding head yes

In the western world, people shake their heads left to right to signal "NO.". They nod their heads up and down to signal "YES." Watch for those occasions when the head movement and words don't match. If that happens, it's a hot spot. This looks natural, but it can signal they don't believe the words they're saying. For example, if someone shakes their head no and says "You can ask me anything." You know that, in fact, they don't want you to ask them anything.

For example, when I asked my husband if he wanted rotisserie chicken for dinner, he shook his head no and said, "That will be okay." We had something different because I caught his lie. I learned later that he was trying to be pleasing and doesn't like rotisserie chicken at all.

People move their heads all the time to accent points. Don't judge every head movement. This is at play frequently but easiest to detect with simple questions that require a yes or no answer.

Hands

Showing palms

How to Detect Lies, Fraud and Identity Theft

When people flash their palms, they're telling their truth—which may or may not always be the truth, but it's the truth under which they are operating. When you're selling something, you need to incorporate their truth into whatever questions or ideas you bring to them. This could be as simple as what they're telling you about their budget or satisfaction with an option on a proposal.

This motion happens really fast and looks very natural so believe it when you see it the first time. The body can't lie.

TRACI BROWN

Hiding Hands

How to Detect Lies, Fraud and Identity Theft

Often, you'll see people in a conversation sit with their hands on the table. When the conversation moves to questions where you need direct answers to tough questions and their hands suddenly move below the table, it's likely they're hiding something and aren't 100% forthcoming with all the information. People hide their hands when they're hiding the truth, and if they're standing, you may see hand-hiding manifest by putting hands in pockets.

> Now you see them, now you don't.
>
> **Tamara Kleinberg— Chief Innovator, Launch Street**
>
> *I sent my 11-year-old boy to school with $40 for the book sale. He came home with a book, a pen, and a wad of cash. When I asked how much he spent, he said $8 for the book and $3 for the pencil. And he handed me $25. I said, "Are you sure you didn't buy anything else? This doesn't add up."*

He said, "No."

I said, "Are you sure? Did you go somewhere after school?"

"We went to Cake Crumbs (our local bakery). But I just bought my friend a Sprite to help him out."

"You didn't get anything for yourself?"

"I wasn't thirsty."

"I'm going to ask you again—the math doesn't add up. What did you get for yourself?"

"I got a Dr Pepper."

It was only $2, but he doesn't get to lie to me, even over that amount. He got in big trouble.

Besides the math being off, I knew he was lying because he tends to come up with ridiculous statements when he's lying. (I wasn't thirsty? You get water when you're thirsty.) And he'll put his hands in his pockets or rub his leg where his pockets should be. He did all these. Pants on fire!

Face

Hiding Lips

Whenever you see people's lips disappear as they're thinking about how they're going to answer your question, the next thing out of their mouth will be, at best, a half-truth, possibly a 100% lie. This is simply rolling lips back over the teeth and is a cousin to covering their mouths with their hands before they answer.

Mouth Covering

People will cover their mouths when they are holding back. If they are directly asked a question and do this, the next thing out of their mouth could be false. If others are speaking and you see this, there's something important on their minds they don't want to say.

Whenever you see someone cover their mouth, further questioning is in order to get to the truth. It happens quickly and can look very natural. But, don't be fooled! Keep asking until you get to the truth. Sometimes saying something as simple as "It seems like you've got more you want to say." Can get them to open up.

Scratching Face

People touch their noses, necks, and faces all the time. During the tough questions, you may see people scratch. Here's why: when people get anxious, blood rushes to the extremities (like the face) in case they need to run. It's the fight-or-flight response. This increase in blood pressure can be the result of anxiety, which may be from telling a lie, or it could be from the situation in general. When blood pressure goes up, tiny facial capillaries dilate, causing them to itch.

When you see this, ask a few unrelated questions to see if they frequently touch their face. If they do, you may just be seeing their typical pattern. If they don't, you may have a liar on your hands. A word of caution: Don't incriminate based on face scratching alone. You'll want to see other signs as well before you make a decision about them telling the truth or not.

Closing Eyes/Covering Face-Mouth

When you see people cover their faces or eyes or even close their eyes during their story about what happened in a certain situation, it can be because they don't want to see the truth (and, that truth may be painful.)

Duper's Delight

What do football player, Tom Brady, and ice skater, Tonya Harding, have in common? In their press conferences, they both displayed dupers delight before denying involvement in their respective crimes.

This is signified by a big smile before answering a potentially very incriminating question. There's nothing happy about the situation or having to answer the question, but they still smile before answering.

When you see this tipoff, it's because deep down inside—below the level they'll admit to—they think they are getting away with the crime and the story they're telling about it. So, watch for that big smile before they answer that tough question.

The Fake Smile or The Pan Am Smile

A closed-mouth smile with no wrinkles around the eyes can be a fake smile. It's done when trying to please and can show submissiveness. It's called the Pan Am smile after the flight attendants on the old Pan Am Airlines. They'd do anything to make you happy.

For lie detection, you'll want to look for those wrinkles around the eyes to see if real emotion is present. Lies are not connected to emotion. The emotion has to be added in by the liar and, many times, will seem either forced or non-existent. For example, is your potential client truly excited about the project they're wanting a loan for? If they're not, you will want to ask more questions to find out why they want the loan before you write them a check.

Feet

Feet Trying to Run but Standing Still

We have the least control over our feet. When people are answering tough questions and are on the spot and have to stay there to answer (like at a press conference or interview), they'll look like they're rocking and fidgeting. This is caused by anxiety and stress. Their unconscious mind is saying "Danger! We've got run!" but their conscious mind says, "We need to stay." The feet try to run, but the body doesn't go anywhere.

This isn't a lying tell in itself but a clue they don't want to be there. And, this can coincide with lying. When seen with other signs, it's another clue that their pants are on fire.

Body

Shrugging Shoulders

A shoulder shrug is a sure tipoff of uncertainty. Watch for this because it coincides with people's words. When you see the shrug, you'll know they're not sure of what they're saying.

Eyes and Eye Patterns

There is a lot of conflicting information about eye patterns as they pertain to lying. What follows is information the FBI interrogators are trained to look for as well as consistencies I've seen over my career working with clients. Some of what I've experienced and learned in the trenches seems to conflict with scientific studies. The details presented here are based on what I've found that works in the everyday world.

Before we start, however, we need to dispel a couple of myths:

MYTH 1

Shifty Eyed people are liars. Not necessarily so. Some people's eyes roll around in their head a lot more than others. They're naturally shifty-eyed. A shift from normal, still eyes to shifty, or shifty to still, can be classified as a "significant shift in behavior." You're looking for the overall behavioral shift, not just the eye pattern itself.

MYTH 2

Liars don't make eye contact. Seems like an unconscious response to guilt, right? This is both right and wrong. As in Myth 1, you're looking for a shift in behavior. Some people have a "look to talk rule"; they will look you in the eye no matter what. Some look you in the eye much less frequently. You've got to take a baseline assessment of their behavior and, when it shifts during the tough questions, then you have a red flag. Some FBI trainers say that all but the good liars will have a hard time making eye contact. Again, don't put all your eggs in this basket.

They say the eyes are the "window to the soul." And, reading people's eye patterns can tell you when and where they're searching for information in their mind before they answer any of your questions. You'll see explanations of what's likely on people's minds as they answer, but the key in lie detection is to notice when people suddenly shift their eye patterns as they give answers during a line of questioning.

For example, when Dr. Phil interviewed Burke Ramsey on his involvement in the death of his sister, Jon Benet, he suddenly shifted from looking down and to the viewer's right just before each answer about what happened that evening to looking down and to the viewer's left when asked point blank "Did you kill Jon Benet?" In this case, that's a big red flag.

Let's dive into what some of these eye patterns can mean. They do have a high degree of accuracy but can't be solely depended upon with every individual. The descriptions below are for a right-handed person. Left-handers can present in the opposite manner but don't always follow that switched pattern. Remember, use this as a guideline, not an absolute rule for everyone.

Looking to the Right

If someone looks to your right as they're putting together their answer to your questions, often they are REMEMBERING. If they look up, they're making a picture of it in their mind before the words come out of their mouths. Similarly, if they look more level to the right, they may be remembering how something sounded.

Looking Down and to the Right

When people look down and to **your** right just before they answer, they are often going through the criteria needed for the answer. They'll often answer with facts, figures, process, and what makes sense. Those in technical jobs like engineers, lawyers, and doctors get their answers from this area frequently.

Looking to the Left

When people look to **your** left just before they answer your question, they are often constructing or fabricating their answer. If they look up, they're making a picture of what they wish would have happened or what something could be like, if they look more level (towards their ear), they can be constructing what something would have sounded like. If they look down and to your left, they are often re-experiencing their feelings about the situation. The feelings are their true feelings.

Defocused Eyes

When you see someone appear to defocus their eyes as they're telling their story, they often are going into a brain space of constructing the image of what they're saying instead of remembering it. That means they're making up what they're saying.

Pacifiers

During tense situations, it's natural to touch one's self to relieve tension. Some of the common ones are:

Cracking knuckles

Hugging one's self

Tapping/drumming fingers

Coughing

Swallowing hard

Clearing your throat

Yawning

Rocking, bouncing, wiggling

Crossing legs (watch for timing on this one)

Hair touching, twirling, or stroking

Self-Grooming & picking

Finger, toe or heel tapping

Sitting on their feet

Hand wringing

Humming/whistling/singing

Everyone does these things. They're very common. But, watch to see if there's a shift. if someone has been open and confident and suddenly shifts to one or more of these, it's a big hot spot. Look for connections between fidgeting/

pacifying and certain words. Figure out their patterns and crack the code. Example: Do they always look down and tap their heels when you talk about stealing?

> Find the Pattern, Find the Lie
>
> **Nora Burns—HR Executive, HR Undercover**
>
> *I was a Human Resources director for a big warehouse. We did 3rd party logistics so we didn't own any of the warehoused goods. In this case, it was mostly yogurt. We were experiencing a higher than normal amount of inventory shrinkage. There's always some shrinkage in a warehouse when pallets get run over by a forklift, etc., but this was way out of normal.*
>
> *Our investigation revealed that it was coming from the weekend overnight shift. When I interviewed the supervisor, he started to fidget and would look down at his left knee. He also had a strange head movement. He said that he didn't know anything about it.*
>
> *We interviewed him again a few days later. But, before he arrived in my office, I had gotten a blank VHS tape and labeled it 3rd Shift Surveillance with the date in question. I put it on a shelf where he'd see it down toward his left knee. I knew he'd look there and I knew he'd see it.*

When asked, again, if he knew anything about the shrinkage and if there was theft going on, he said "I might know where a few cases went." He said that people were just walking out the door with them.

We got permission from the CEO to shake people down a bit. We had them go out to the parking lot and stand by the car that they arrived in and pop the trunk. And, there we found where the yogurt was going—home with most of the employees, including the supervisor.

VERBAL TELLS

You can get more with a kind word and a gun than with a kind word alone.

—Al Capone

Body language and words combine to create the true meaning of your communication. In the same manner that you learn to recognize body language hot spots, words and word patterns can be very revealing.

Remember, you want to compare people to themselves. Words have several components to listen for. Start by baselineing people and notice when people show significant shifts. Here are a few speech qualities to learn to listen for:

Tone

Tone is one of the most reliable indicators of deception. After all, it's not about what they say, but how they said it.

Tone rises when people are excited and angry. It lowers with sadness and shame.

One of the most important tones to listen for is convincing versus conveying. Liars will try to convince you and may adopt a slightly angry and forceful tone. Truthful folks convey information in a much more peaceful manner. Truthful people don't feel like they need to prove anything.

Another telltale sign of lying is a complete lack of emotion in the tone. We heard this from Ryan Lochte recounting the events of being robbed at the Olympics. He used a totally deadpan tone, which he later admitted. Pants on fire!

> It's not what you said, it's how you said it.
>
> **Beth Ziesenis—Professional Tech Guru—Your Nerdy Friend**
>
> *I caught my practice-husband cheating, and for several months, we went back and forth with counseling and promises and ranting and tears. He swore that he wasn't talking to her anymore and that he was with me forever.*
>
> *One day, I found a mobile device in the trunk of our car. "Why do you have a cell phone?" I asked.*
>
> *"It's not a phone. It's a radio for work."*
>
> *"That's a phone! It's a phone! You're talking to her again!"*
>
> *"No, I swear to you. It's not a phone."*
>
> *His voice quality changed. He barked. He cussed. He*

threw the phone back into the trunk and slammed the lid. I had never seen him so angry.

"Get in the [bleep]-ing car!"

I was scared to say anything.

We had a 30-mile drive, and we were excruciatingly quiet. I was crying.

When he pulled into the driveway, we both sat there.

Quietly I said, "We both know that's not a radio. You're lying to me. We both know it."

He said nothing.

"I don't deserve to be lied to." I was so quiet I was surprised he heard me.

"No, you don't," he said, almost as quietly.

We went inside and didn't speak of the phone again. The next weekend, I went on a planned trip with a girlfriend. When I returned, he had left a note on the counter. I've never seen or talked to him again.

[PS—no empathy needed. The guy did me a favor by leaving. I'm incredibly happy now. I wasn't then.]

Other Voice Quality Indicators to Listen For

For the rest of this list, none of these are any better indicators of deception than the others. Once you've baselined someone, listen for shifts with these qualities:

Tempo—Pace of speech. Are they slow or fast like an auctioneer?

Volume—How loud are they?

Pitch—It can vary from deep to squeaky.

Timing—How quickly do they answer you? Some people are late responders (more than three seconds) but not most. People who pause too long after the question are often liars.

Rhythm—Hesitation and stumbling versus smooth.

Level of responsiveness—Some people are quiet; others will talk your ear off.

Clarity—Crisp versus mumble. We all mumble sometimes. Increase in mumbling can indicate lying.

Verbal Patterns Liars Will Show

Answering unasked questions

Professional liars will try to get ahead of you and direct the conversation. If the answer is lengthy, it's a hot spot.

When people challenge your question

> *"Why are you asking me that?" or "That's a dumb question, why are you asking me that?" or "Do I have to answer?"*

Stalling

> *If they repeat the question back to you or ask for clarification—it's usually a lie.*

Anger

> *How do you tell real anger from fake? Give it some time. Fake anger will run out of steam. Real anger will turn to rage. Some will misplace the anger and get angry at the interviewer. It's like shooting the messenger and can be a sign of deception.*

Truthful people don't negotiate the truth

> *Detectives will test a suspect by asking "Just to make it go away, will you buy this guy a new truck?" If he says yes, he's negotiating … and lying.*

Automatic and planned responses

> *When they start their answer with "I knew you'd ask" or "Good question" or "I'm going to say this again"'*

Well…

> *When answers to yes or no questions start with "'Well…" they're lying.*

Speech error rate

> *We all have errors in our speech. It goes up during a lie.*

Qualifying their Story

> *When the answer begins with "You're not going to believe this, but …" or "This is going to sound strange, but …" or "I know this is outta left field …" don't believe it!*

Anything other than a no is a yes.

> *"Did you hit your brother?" "I didn't hurt him."*

Evasive responses

> *If answering a yes or no question with "Maybe," it's a hot spot.*

Watch out if they tell you how great they are; they're liars.

It's All in the Timing

Alex Hearn—Bikerpelli Sports

I run an adventure outdoor company. We run large supported four-day mountain biking trips along the Kokopelli trail from Fruita, Colorado to Moab, Utah. It takes lots of training to complete the ride and it's not for the meek even if you are fit.

Every year, about a week before the trip begins, there are a rash of "injuries." I get calls reporting everything from broken collarbones and legs to cancer. These are long after the cancellation refund date. I know these people haven't trained and are just trying to get their money back. I ask them to send a picture of themselves and their x-ray along with today's newspaper (so I can see the date) and they always go silent.

Marie Jenkinson—Owner, Lionsgate Event Center

We had a wedding that took place at the Gatehouse between an older couple, maybe in their 40s. They were okay through planning but not one of our more loved couples. My son is also a great wedding photographer and was hired to shoot their wedding. He was in the bride's room before the wedding taking the "getting ready" shots and the bride, her sister, and her sister's two girls (about 3 and 5 years old) were there. The bride's sister wanted shots of the girls jumping on the bed (which we do quite a lot—cute photos of them laughing in midair, etc.). Wedding and reception went fine.

My son said they were okay throughout the taking of photos and had some ideas of shots they liked but mostly wanted him to do candid photos; they were very unconcerned about the photography part. After the wedding, my son started editing the images and started posting them on a private site where the bride and groom have a security login and can start reviewing the images.

I got a call from the bride's sister (on my cell phone, which is also the emergency number for the business).

She doesn't say who she is or what her call is in regards to but starts yelling at me about how one of our photographers has published child pornography on a public website of her daughter and she is going to call the police.

WOW! I was totally shocked and tried my best to calm her down and get the info on who she is and what she was talking about. Finally discovered who she was and the photos she was yelling about. My son had copied me on some of the photos as he thought they were turning out really cute, so I had seen some of them already and knew what she was talking about.

Turns out that two of the photos of the girls jumping on the bed were shot when her youngest daughter was falling on the bed and her crotch was showing a bit. She had underwear and white tights on, so it wasn't obvious that this might be considered an inappropriate image. Anyway, I couldn't get her to calm down much and only told her that I would be sure those two images would be taken down immediately and tried to assure her that this was NOT a public website, and only her sister had access to it (she had been yelling that now THOUSANDS of people have seen her daughter's crotch).

We ended up finding out that she did call the police to report child pornography but were told that the image was not pornographic and she couldn't do anything. Then her sister, the bride, starts emailing my son telling him how upset she is with the other wedding photos, that some are out of focus (he was using depth of field where the person in the foreground was clear and then it is blurry in the background—like all good photographers do) and that he took photos of people while they were talking, etc. (she wanted candid photos).

In the end, she was so unreasonable and he didn't want to deal with her anymore that he refunded her 100% of the money and still gave her all the images.

In the end, we usually get more lies after the wedding, where people are searching for something to complain about in hopes of getting money back.

INTERROGATION TECHNIQUES: HOW TO FIND THE TRUTH

Lying is a delightful thing for it leads to the truth.
—Fyodor Dostoevsky, *Crime and Punishment*

You're pretty sure someone is lying. Use these tactics to uncover the truth. But, first, ask yourself if it's worth it. Sometimes it's okay to just know someone is lying. It's okay to let them get away with it and not let them know that you know they're lying until it's worth it. You gotta pick your battles.

Tactics to Get to the Truth

You will want to use these tactics at different times, based on the situation. Yes, some of these conflict. There's a situation to use each. Don't be afraid to switch between them if you're not getting the information you want.

Uncovering lies can be as simple as having them tell their story, then asking "What happened before that?" They have to stop and create the answer, and you may see some of the response patterns above. If their answer doesn't quite fit, ask an unrelated question and come back to it to see if the response is the same.

Verbal Patterns

Use the softer word to describe a problem.

With '"stole" vs "took," use took. It sounds more innocent and puts less pressure on the interviewee.

Ask closed-ended questions.

Ask questions that require a yes or no answer. Not "Is there anything else I should know about?" Then use this "rule of thumb": any other answer than no means yes. Any answer other than yes means no.

Don't ask too much at once; ask about small chunks.

"What did you do Friday night?" vs. "Did you go out Friday night?"

"Help me out here, I'm confused."

Use this to get people to retell their story in greater detail. The details will provide opportunities to ask questions and find any inconsistencies or truth.

Listen for gradients within the same topic.

"Uh, not really" is different than "no way." If there's no real change within the story, it's either all lies or all truth.

Your Demeanor

Be stoic; don't show emotion during interrogation

Don't leak when you believe or not. Liars will work to embellish their story. Give them enough rope, and they'll hang themselves.

Be nonjudgmental

Don't show disdain. Liars will shut down if they think you're against them.

Agree with them/side with them.

It's the suspects that need to tell the truth. Interrogators don't need to tell the truth to get clients to confess. Agreeing with your suspect can help lead them down the path to tell you more and make it seem okay to admit what they did. You have to be a good actor to pull this off.

Environment Set Up

Sit with your back to a blank wall.

Force them to pay attention and not zone out on things in the room.

Take away the desk/table between you.

Put chairs 3.5 feet apart. It's easier to tell when they're lying. Liars feel safer behind a desk. Make sure chairs are firm but comfortable, not twisty; no wheels or springy back to absorb movements.

Give them at least 18 inches of separation from you.

If you get into their space too much, it can make them nervous, and nervous signs can be misinterpreted as lies.

Ask questions one on one.

There's more truth told one on one than with a panel.

Make the room bright.

People are less likely to lie in bright environments.

Sometimes just change your approach…

Mary Kelly—Economist and Retired Chief of Police, Naval Air Station, Hawaii

All my good lying stories are from when I was the chief of police because everyone has an incentive to lie. They think they won't get caught or that you will be stupid or not thorough. And, in some cases, they're right; so, you must be careful.

When I got to work one morning all dressed up in my Navy whites, I walked into my office, and my petty officer walked in, shaking his head, very frustrated, and said, "We've got a doozy in holding room 1." He said, "She tried to jump off a building; she's drunk and belligerent; she won't tell us her real name."

I said, "What have you gotten out of her?"

He said, "Nothing, Ma'am, just that she lives on base and is a military spouse. She had a bad night and anything she's told us is a lie."

That's typical because I knew that lots of times when people are in the wrong they want to minimize the consequences.

I walk in the room with my cup of coffee. This holding room is like a hotel room. And, at some point during the night she'd decided to jump in the shower. Here she is, this wet, soggy, mass of sadness sitting on the couch crying and shaking. Instead of sitting at the table like an interrogation, I gave her a look, sat down on the couch with my coffee and didn't say anything. I knew she had to stop crying eventually. She was having body-shuddering sobs (like little kids) that stopped when she realized she wasn't really getting any attention or sympathy. When she gathered herself, she said "What are you doing here?".

I said, "Just having coffee." I sipped my coffee.

Keep in mind, when people are in a stressful situation

and they're going to lie, not being able to blurt out that lie quickly actually messes with their heads and creates lots of uncertainty. That's why "Just wait till your father gets home" is very effective with kids.

After a couple more minutes, I looked over and said, "Rough night, huh?" And, she burst into tears and sobs again. I said, "So, what are you doing here?" And then, she told me ... everything—more than I wanted to know about her history being an abused child and more.

My cops had only asked her "What's your name ... what's going on?" Only direct questions. And, I just went in casually with my coffee and started to get the answers.

She said, "Well, my husband is coming back from deployment and I've been unfaithful so I got really drunk and then I slept with one of his friends and then I felt worse so I tried to jump off a building and kill myself" ... on and on.

I said, "We're going to solve some of those problems." (The military has great support for folks like her)

Simply changing the approach sometimes gets you to the truth like it did this time.

Getting to the Truth

Mary Kelly—Economist and Retired Chief of Police, Naval Air Station, Hawaii

I had one other tactic to get to the truth. I'd work to take away motivation, incentive, and opportunity to lie. I'd go in with coffee because, for some reason, I'd get different responses when I had coffee versus water. Coffee is sort of comforting and instills confidence. I'd sit down with a suspect and say "so ... we're just going to have a conversation and try to figure out what's going on."

When you're talking to a suspect, which is what a lot of people don't realize, is that we (the cops) don't have to tell the truth. The suspect is supposed to tell the truth. But, until we have a signed statement, nothing they say really counts. I would go in casually and say we're just going to talk because I'm a little confused and I'm hoping you can help me. This is powerful because people shift from being defensive to being a little more knowledgeable.

Then I'd say. "I'm kind of embarrassed, but have you heard of ESP and psychics?" They'd always say "yeah." I'd say I'm not really a psychic and I don't really have ESP and I know this sounds crazy but, when I look at people and they're lying to me, it's like a big red light goes off in their heads and I just have to say something about it. And I've always been able to do this. I can just see it pulsating in people's brains. Apparently, other people can't see it, but I just wanted to let you know. If I see the light, I'm just going to stop you right there. Because we're both busy people."

By this time, they're totally thrown off guard. So, now, I have a whole lie going and they're freaked out because they don't know if their lie is going to work. But, they invariably try it. I'd say something like:

"Tony said he saw you at the 7-11 last night at 2 am."

They'd say "that wasn't me. I wasn't there."

Then I'd say "I'm starting to get the red light on a little blink, which means you're thinking about lying. So, can you tell me a little bit more about where you were?" And they would. And then, we'd get to the good stuff where I knew they were lying. I could tell by their body language. Often, I'd say "Ooo, that light is going off. Can you start over ... and don't lie this time?" Then they would tell me the truth!

Some of those stories are crazy…

Alan Berg—Wedding Business Guru and Professional Speaker

We were renting out a townhouse (which we weren't able to sell when we moved 100 miles away) to a family. We were constantly chasing him for the rent. Every month it was another lie. He always paid, but always late, sometimes days, sometimes weeks, or even months (he was on time 4 times in 4 years).

There was always an excuse, and the tip off was that it was always someone else's fault (his boss, his secretary, he's waiting for a commission check, etc.). He never took responsibility for being late. There was a late fee, and once he was late, and the fee was assessed, he'd feel no pressure to pay soon, as he acted as if the fee were a free pass to just pay the following month.

When I'd call him out on the lies, he'd get very indignant (wasn't it Shakespeare, who said, "Methinks thou doth protest too much?"), and then the lies would snowball, and, as you said in your blog, the details and his indignation were part of the tipoff. We didn't care about why. We only cared that he was late, again.

His company did work with the government and

private sector, so sometimes it was that they were waiting to get paid by the government agency; other times, it was that he was waiting on his bonus; then it was that he asked his secretary to make the deposit and she left too late or left the check at the office (he would deposit directly into my account at a branch). It was always something.

…and they'll tell you too much

Kevin Jamison—Lawyer

People lie to me all the time. The first lie is they will pay me. I remember one client who insisted they were not that kind of person and would never never stiff me. (She did.) Being over-insistent about something is a bad sign.

Many lie about alibis. I have been assured on many occasions that the client was elsewhere when something happened. People I cannot reach or find or perhaps never existed are advanced to support the alibi. I can almost see the wheels turning while they decide what would be to their benefit and believable. And, yes, I found later that they were lying. I find sex offenders harder to catch in these lies.

HOW TO DETECT LIES, FRAUD AND IDENTITY THEFT

People who talk very fast and continuously are lying. I saw this in my law practice and also when I operated a liquor store. These people came in my store trying to get me to buy stolen goods (I found a sticker from the Kansas City School System on a computer a guy tried to sell. He gave specifics on the retail store where he bought it, but was vague on what programs he ran on it.) Sometimes they are trying to sell me a bill of goods; an alibi; a story of how things went. They talk fast and constantly so I don't have time to think about what they are telling me, much less ask questions.

Stories often change depending on what the client thinks I want to hear.

HOW TO DETECT IDENTITY THEFT AND FRAUD

*The biggest lie ever: I have read and
agree to the terms of use.*

The crimes we hear so much about these days are usually cyber crimes—someone intercepts a wire transfer for your mortgage down payment or opens a credit card, online, in your name and goes on an internet shopping spree. What we don't hear about is how much financial crime happens in person.

There are countless incidents of in-person fraud and identity theft. Folks who aren't who they say they are go into banks all the time and apply for credit cards, apply for loans, and open accounts. Payday loan stores give loans to people who fake their identity all the time. Business owners who actually are who they say they are may show up to their loan appointment with a fake profit-and-loss statement.

How can you detect identity thieves that are right in front of you?

According to master interrogator, Stan Slowik, ask a string of questions that are increasingly more complex that only the actual person will know. Hopefully, you already know the answers to them. If you notice hot spots as the questions get more challenging, they may not be who they say they are. If you don't see any hot spots, their answers are either all true or all lies. According to Stan, what shifts the most as the questions get more detailed is their timing.

The actual person should have spontaneous answers to questions like, "Where do you live now?" "Where did you live in the past?" "What's your mom's maiden name?" and "What's your dog's name?"

Fortunately, many of these types of questions are on any application. If the application is on paper, get them to fill it out and, then, just casually verify the answers when you talk with them. And if you start up a friendly conversation to add in some extra questions, that helps, too. Here's how a conversation could play out:

> Name. How do you spell that?
>
> Spouse name? And how do you spell that?
>
> Address? How do you spell that street and what's the zip again? I can't quite read your writing.
>
> Can you confirm your birthday?
>
> What's your social security number?

During conversation, be sure to say things like, "How many kids do you have? Oh, I have kids, too. What grade are your's in?"

How to Detect Lies, Fraud and Identity Theft

IMPORTANT: If you're taking their information verbally and typing it into the computer, make sure you look at them! It's easy to bury your head behind the screen. If you do that, you'll miss the hot spots in their reaction.

The complex questions get easier to ask with business loans. Of course, you'll ask the standard info. But, drilling down on the details of how they're going to pay you back will be revealing. Some of the questions could include:

> What are your profit margins the last three years?
>
> How are you going to cover the costs of having two offices since you're moving out during the renovation?
>
> How exactly are you going to get the business to support your new expanded manufacturing capacity?

Taking the time to drill deep into the complexities of who a person is or how they plan to use the money you loan them will show everything you need to know about the real level of risk you're taking.

Are they really who they say they are?

Luis Tavel—Professional Speaker, former Police Officer

One story that sticks in my mind is from early 2009, during a trip to San Diego to a film festival for work. I HAD to spend a torturous 10 days in San Diego in February and I had already been there three days. The hotel bar served the best pesto chicken sandwich on the planet, and I was yet again at the bar for lunch with a co-worker, enjoying one.

We struck up a conversation with a guy, who seemed nice and personable—almost too nice for my taste, and so, my former cop-mind perked up and I started asking myself what was wrong with the picture.

It became obvious he was lying when I asked where he was from—you know, him being at a hotel and all—and he said Colorado. I told him, so was I, and inquired whereabouts in Colorado he was from... "Denver" he said. Me: Denver is a big place ... I said "Denver, south Denver? Downtown? Littleton?" Him: "Yes, Littleton!" I said "Cool, I grew up in Littleton. Where in Littleton?" Him: "You know, right in the middle." Me: "Okay...like near Columbine?" Him: "Yeah, right there!" Me: "Oh, yeah...I love that area of town ... what's the name of the park right there?" I asked that, knowing that anyone from near Columbine would know the name Clement Park. Of course, he had no idea and I decided to end the conversation shortly after that.

A few minutes later, there were two San Diego Police officers standing behind him who proceeded to arrest him. Turns out, he was staying at the hotel on a stolen identity and paying for everything with a stolen credit card.

Thankfully, I didn't accept his offer to buy my buddy and me a drink.

SO YOU FOUND A LIAR—WHAT NEXT?

Our lies reveal as much about us as our truths.
—J. M. Coetzee, *Slow Man*

When you know you've got a liar on your hands, the situation will dictate what you do next.

Hopefully, they've admitted it. But, if they haven't, and they're not going to, you have three choices:

1. Let it go. You don't have to make every lie an issue. Many times, for small lies, it's easier to file your knowledge away until the time that it becomes important. Maybe that's never. But pick your battles. Not everything is worth a confrontation.

2. Do something about it but don't tell them. For example, if you know your husband doesn't want rotisserie chicken for dinner, get something else. You don't need to bring it up. You can really make his day by getting something else you know he'd like.

3. Do your homework to expose the lie. Due diligence is especially important in banking and finance. If you suspect someone is misrepresenting themselves or their financial status, dig deeper and find the evidence. It's in the paperwork and records some-

where. Inattention and laziness makes you a target for fraud loss.

In personal life, you may have a tougher time gathering evidence. But if you suspect something, keep your mouth shut and keep looking. Where there's smoke, there's fire. Evidence will reveal itself.

How to Get an Admission

When you remove the chance they can get away with it, you'll often get others to admit their lie. As we heard from Mark Kelly, yes, you can lie to get them to admit theirs. Saying you have evidence (even without showing it to them) can lead to a quick admission.

FINAL REVIEW AND TIPS

And after all, what is a lie? 'Tis but the truth in masquerade.
—Lord Byron

Decide to Survive! It can be tough out there in the wild. Lie detection techniques can be easy to learn but tough to apply. Deception detection is part art and part science. Take the time to get good at it. Body language, words, tone, and timing combine to reveal lies *and* the truth.

Lies come in several forms including Exaggeration, Fabrication, Minimization, Omission, and Deceptive Denial.

No matter what kind of lie you're sniffing out, remember these three things:

1. Pay Attention. The signs are there. The question is, are you watching?
2. Never incriminate on one element of behavior. Look for shifts in behavior at key points in any conversation. When you raise your sensory acuity (that's how much you're paying attention to everything around), you may see hot spots. Clusters of hot spots are much more important and revealing than one hot spot alone.

3. Believe other's communication the first time. You may not get the chance to confirm a lie the 2nd time. The first time someone lies to you it's shame on them. The 2nd time is shame on you!

When you want to practice lie detection and don't want to stare down your friends or co-workers, watch the evening news, reality TV and talk shows—anywhere people are filmed candidly. You'll be amazed at what you see when you watch with trained eyes.

Before taking issue with anyone, ask yourself if it's really worth it. You may save time and energy by just letting it go. When you know more than what comes out of your and their mouths, you have true power.

ABOUT THE AUTHOR

Question: What do Lance Armstrong, Chris Christie and Vladimir Putin have in common?

Answer: Traci Brown's revealed their secrets to the world.

And she's told the world what they're not saying. NBC, CBS and Fox have asked this body language expert to reveal secrets hidden in plain sight.

And she can help your team reveal the secrets your clients are keeping from you that are impacting your bottom line.

Traci has even adapted the skills to talk herself out of an embarrassing number of traffic tickets and into lucrative deals. She'll teach you how to do it, too!

Traci's system landed her a lucrative product deal with Kevin Harrington, a Shark from ABC's hit show Shark Tank and took her on a wild ride to the big time consumer markets of TV shopping channels, infomercials and beyond.

She speaks globally. In her fast paced, interactive programs that are sure to entertain, Traci teaches high performance persuasion that worked to get the deal with her Shark.

You'll be able to immediately use the same tools to create more success in your own organization and personal life…so you see more zeroes (before the decimal) in your bank account.

Traci is a Three Time US Collegiate Cycling Champion and former member of Team USA. Yeah, she's fast on 2 wheels and looks pretty good in spandex. And just ask her how she used body language to win bike races. Yep, it's true.

She is the past president of the National Speaker's Association Colorado Chapter and the author of three books, Persuasion Point, Body Language Confidential and Body Language for Profits.

She lives in Boulder, CO with her rocket scientist husband and her Siberian Husky.

Book Traci for your next conference or meeting!

BodyLanguageTrainer.com